M000072824

I have always felt that we don't give enough credence to Easter as a High Holy Day. By understanding the personal lives of those close to the Savior, I am much better prepared to put myself into the celebration with a more personal and holy mind-set. (Marsha K.)

*Celebrating a Christ-Centered Easter* is the perfect go-to book for finding new family traditions that will bring you and your family closer to Jesus Christ this holiday. (Alysha B.)

This Easter book helps us see through the eyes of others the love Jesus Christ has for us and how the small things are important. It brings a beautiful spirit, in a very simple way, that will help people of all ages make Jesus Christ the center of the Easter season. (Teri G.)

I came away from these pages with more gratitude for my Savior, and I'm excited to use these traditions to remember Him through this special time of the year. (Christine M.)

This is a book for everyone looking to bring Jesus Christ into their homes, and to celebrate the experiences and love Easter brings. (Korrine C.)

This is a great book—not only for a more meaningful Easter season, but for ideas that will help carry the spirit of Easter in our hearts throughout the year. (Brittany A.)

This will be a treasured book in our home. From the stories to the activities, it will be something we can do any time of year to help us remember Jesus Christ. (Beckie S.)

As Emily Freeman lays out the things those in the Savior's life went through during the time surrounding His death, she helps us to experience their emotions and the lessons they learned. She has a gift for applying the scriptures to our daily lives. (Megan W.)

If you have ever felt like your Easter celebrations have been missing something, this is the book for you. (Lisa E.)

A beautiful story of the rich yet simple interactions of the humble followers of Jesus in the weeks prior to the first Easter. (Linda A.)

This book will help you truly take Easter and its full meaning into your heart—not just for a day, but for your whole life. (Barbara C.)

Emily Freeman brings the stories of the people closest to the Savior to life. She gives practical ideas and applications to help others increase their personal relationship with Jesus Christ. (Jennifer B.)

*Celebrating a Christ-Centered Easter* leaves me ready to dig deeper into the scriptures and see if I too can't discover myself on the road to Emmaus. (Ruthann W.)

CELEBRATING A
# Christ-Centered
## Easter

CELEBRATING A

# CHRIST-CENTERED
## Easter

SEVEN TRADITIONS TO LEAD US
CLOSER TO JESUS CHRIST

# EMILY BELLE FREEMAN

ENSIGN
PEAK

*For Nish*
*Whose great love for this High Holiday has deepened mine*

Text © 2015 Emily Belle Freeman

Illustrations © 2015 Jay Ward

Visit us at EnsignPeakPublishing.com

**Library of Congress Cataloging-in-Publication Data**
Freeman, Emily, 1969–    author.
    Celebrating a Christ centered Easter : seven traditions to lead us closer to Jesus Christ / Emily Belle Freeman.
        pages cm
    Includes bibliographical references.
    ISBN 978-1-60907-977-2 (paperbound)
1. Easter.  2. Jesus Christ—Resurrection.  I. Title.
    BV55.F74 2015
    263'.93—dc23                                                2014034323

Printed in the United States of America
Edwards Brothers Malloy, Ann Arbor, MI

10  9  8  7  6  5  4  3  2

# CONTENTS

# ACKNOWLEDGMENTS

It has been my experience that every book, before it is bound, is inspired by the influence and imagination of far more people than just the one who penned the words. This book is no different. Now, therefore, the gratitude.

To Nish Weiseth, whose friendship has made me a better Christian.

To Michael Wilcox, who introduced me to the Easter Sermon and whose deep faith has inspired many cherished conversations.

To the women from South Mountain Community Church—Sarah, Amy, Gini, Kris, Marie, Erica, Laura, Lindsey, Bobbie, Jackie, Jenn, Heather, Lori, Nikole, Abby,

Rachel, Jenny, Myrna, and Tasha. Studying the Bible with you is one of my favorite pastimes.

To Steevun and Tami Lemon for your enthusiasm and believing support in this pursuit.

To Jay Ward; this project would not have been what it is without you. Gratitude for your gift; thankful heart for your timing.

To Emily Watts, without whom I honestly could not survive. My dear friend, confidante, and editor. Thank you for understanding my heart.

To Richard Erickson, Sheryl Dickert Smith, Shauna Gibby, and Kayla Hackett, for your patience with my imagination and the skill and talent with which you bring each dream to life. To Malina Grigg, for inserting changes up to the very last second, and for making every word fit.

To Chris Schoebinger, whose vision has illuminated my life in ways I would never have imagined possible. Thank you for leading me down roads I would never have walked had I not met you.

And, last, to Greg, Caleb, Josh, Garett, Ian, Steven, Megan, and Grace, who have led me to know Jesus Christ. I see Him reflected in each one of you. Thank you for contributing to the experiences that are my life. You are the reason for the joy in every morning and the gratitude that fills my heart when I climb into bed at night. You are my life.

*I know that ye seek Jesus,*
*which was crucified.*
*He is not here:*
*for he is risen.*

MATTHEW 28:5–6, KJV

# INTRODUCTION

I t was just before the Passover. She stood quietly in the crowded room of the house in Bethany, holding an alabaster box in her hands. The ointment inside the box was extremely expensive—she had brought her finest as an offering to the Lord. Humbly, she stood behind Him and broke open the box, carefully pouring the precious oil on His head.

There were some in the room who stood back and watched this tender act of devotion and openly ridiculed her behavior. They wondered why the precious ointment was wasted, complaining that it should have been sold for the more than three hundred pence it was worth. They suggested that the money should have been given to the poor.

I can't help but wonder what thoughts filled this humble woman's heart in that moment. Did she question her devotion? Did she second-guess the action prompted by her adoration? I think not. Her outward expression reflected a sacred inward belief. With deepest gratitude, Jesus said of her offering, "*She hath done what she could: she is come aforehand to anoint my body to the burying. Verily I say unto you, Wheresoever this gospel shall be preached throughout the whole world, this also that she hath done shall be spoken of for a memorial of her*" (Mark 14:8–9, KJV).

What is it about this woman's humble act of devotion that makes it so memorable? Perhaps it is her unwavering devotion to that which she believed, even in the face of mockery. But I think there is more. I love the line that tells us "*she did what she could*" (Mark 14:6, NIV). Her heart was filled to overflowing with adoration for the Lord and deep reverence for the sacrifice He was about to perform. That sentiment defined her actions.

Is the same true of us? Consider your own life for a moment. When was the last time you broke open the alabaster box? Every time I read the story of this humble woman, deep yearning fills my soul. I want to understand the heart of this woman. I want to find a way to express my love to the Savior as she did. I want to be able to say *I have done what I could* for the Lord.

It is Easter. This is a season when we reflect on the suffering, sacrifice, and resurrection of Jesus Christ. It is a moment when we too can break open the alabaster box as we prepare beforehand for this holy celebration.

Perhaps as you feel Easter approaching you find yourself wishing you could do things differently. Maybe you hope to find a way to prepare more fully for the sacred celebration ahead. Recently, I was talking with a friend about her traditions and worship services surrounding this holiday. She referred to Easter as her "high holiday." I pondered her sentiment and knew I wanted Easter to become more of a high holiday in my life and in my home.

I was reminded that Jewish tradition sets aside a certain number of days each year for celebrating. They refer to these days as "High Holidays" or "High Holy Days." In Hebrew the term is *Yamim Noraim*, which means "Days of Awe." That is my heart's desire: I want the days surrounding Easter to become days of awe—high holy days.

For many years our family has celebrated a Christ-centered Christmas. In the seven weeks leading up to Christmas, we learn about the Savior's birth and celebrate a tradition in honor of each of the people whose characters fill the nativity. We decided to celebrate Easter in a similar fashion. This book explains how we celebrate a Christ-centered Easter, but it is different from other Easter books you will read. Most Easter books center on events, on what happened each day of the last week of the Savior's life. This book focuses on the people who were closest to the Savior and spent precious time with Him during the last weeks of His mortal ministry. Instead of events, this book is driven by experiences—one-on-one, personal experiences with Jesus Christ.

The chapters of this book will focus on seven

different personal experiences that took place just before and just after the Lord's suffering, sacrifice, and resurrection. These seven experiences have one thing in common—each of the stories is a personal witness of the Lord's individualized ministry.

In our family we set aside the Sundays before Easter to reflect on the stories of these people who were some of the closest associates of Jesus Christ. As we celebrate each of their stories, we participate in a tradition that will help us to understand the lesson that story teaches about our own personal relationship with the Savior. These traditions fill our home with Easter decorations that symbolize the lessons. Each person has a story to tell, and each has a lesson to share. Studying their experiences has given our family a greater understanding and a deeper appreciation for the miracles that surround the celebration we call Easter.

You might choose to do these traditions in seven days, or you might set aside one night a week for the six weeks leading up to Easter. The order of the traditions and the length of time between each one is left completely to your inspiration. Invite anyone you choose to celebrate these moments with you. The stories and traditions are appropriate for any age and families of any size.

Perhaps now is a good time to tell you about a wish I have had for many years. I am a lover of Christmas nativities. If you were to walk into my home during the Christmas holidays, you would find yourself surrounded by crèches. Every year when Easter approaches I find myself wanting to pull out my nativities. They are such a symbol of the high holiday of Christmas in my heart that it seems they should be a part of this high holiday of Easter also. So we decided to create our own Easter scene. The people whose stories are included in this book are all parts of that Easter scene.

In our family, our Easter scene plays an important role. At the end of the evening, after each story has been told and the tradition has been completed, one person from the family is chosen to add the figurine we studied to the Easter scene. Week by week we begin to fill the scene, one figure at a time, until finally it is complete. The Easter scene becomes an advent calendar of sorts.

As we add each figure to the scene we count down the days until Easter, and our hearts are drawn closer to Jesus Christ. The figure of Christ is always last, placed carefully in the center of the scene on Easter morning.

You might find it helpful to set aside a quiet moment to read through this book before your Easter celebrations begin. Perhaps you would like to highlight certain passages to share out loud at the time you celebrate each tradition. As you read you will quickly discover that the traditions in this book can be implemented in any order—this will allow you to decide what will work best for your circumstances.

I grew up reading the King James Version of the Bible, and to this day, whenever I hear the language of that book of scripture, my soul is home. As I have grown older, my study of the Bible has included master teachers such as Frederic Farrar and Alfred Edersheim, as well as many different translations of the Bible. The New International Version happens to be one of my favorite translations. The initial translation of the NIV was accomplished with constant reference to the Hebrew,

Aramaic, and Greek manuscripts in an effort to remain faithful to the original languages as the Bible was translated into its English style. Over the years I have found that the combination of these two translations has proved to be very beneficial in my personal study. This Easter book makes reference to those two translations of the Bible accordingly. The emphasis added with italics in the scriptures quoted is mine unless otherwise indicated.

My thoughts are with you as we enter this season of hope and celebration. May those two emotions become the guiding principles behind this experience. Hope for an Easter filled with the Spirit of Christ and feelings of celebration as we offer our finest to Him in deepest gratitude for His sacrifice.

Prepare to experience days of awe.

Break open the alabaster box.

*The Spirit of the Lord God is upon me;*
*because the Lord hath anointed me*
*to preach good tidings unto the meek . . .*

ISAIAH 61:1, KJV

# ONE

# LAZARUS

For most people, the event that signals the beginning of Easter week is the Lord's triumphal entry into Jerusalem. One thing I love most about that story is the donkey. For centuries the crowds in Jerusalem had anticipated the arrival of a Messiah who would deliver them, and perhaps the image they had foreseen included a white stallion and a sword. But such was not to be the case. Yes, Jesus Christ, the Messiah, would deliver them—just not in the way they had anticipated. In fact, everything about His deliverance was unexpected, from the humble man of simple circumstance who entered Jerusalem on a donkey to His final hours on the cross on Calvary. It was deliverance so unexpected that many didn't even realize it had taken place.

We could focus on the triumphal entry, on the spontaneous celebration surrounding that unexpected event, but this is a book that celebrates people, and so instead, our journey will begin with a personal encounter with the Lord—an unexpected encounter that took place just shortly before the triumphal entry into Jerusalem.

It had been four days—four dark days of weeping, of wondering, and of asking why.

"If you had been here . . ." Martha whispered to the Lord as she ran to meet Him on the dusty road in front of her home. "If you had been here . . ." Mary echoed and then fell down at His feet, the grief too much for her physical frame to bear. Sorrow overflowing, still she clung to her faith in Him. He saw the tears streaming down her face, streaming down the faces of the friends who had come to mourn, and Jesus wept. "If you believed,"

He pled with them, "you would see" (John 11:21, 32, 40, NIV).

They took away the stone from the place where the dead man lay. Then Jesus prayed, and the Father heard, and Jesus cried with a loud voice, "Lazarus, come forth" (John 11:43, KJV).

Come forth from the darkness.

Come forth from the mourning, the sorrow, and the anguish.

Come forth from that which holds you back . . . and be healed.

And so, still bound with grave clothes hand and foot, his face covered with the napkin, Lazarus came forth. He whom Christ loved was risen from the dead.

The scriptures do not tell us what happened afterward; we can only imagine the celebration that surely followed, the gratitude and the awe. What we do know is that this miracle of miracles marked one of the highest points in the ministry of Jesus Christ up to that moment in His mortal life. It was an experience that symbolized the hope in which His disciples believed—and it solidified the hatred of those who sought to bring His mission to an end.

The miracle was an unforeseen answer to a call for help that had been expressed by two sisters four days before. It came when every human condition would suggest it shouldn't have. In the darkest moment. Unexpectedly.

I wonder if you have ever found yourself in a similar circumstance. Maybe you have cried out to the Lord in anguish from a dark place. Perhaps you know about the waiting and the wondering that come in those moments when you question if the Lord has forgotten you. It's not that you don't have faith. It's just that sometimes it feels as if the timing of the miracle you are pleading for goes unanswered. We must remember that sometimes the miracle we are hoping for is not the miracle the Lord holds in store. Sometimes miracles come in unexpected ways, and they come in the Lord's timing rather than in ours.

And yet, the Lord is constantly aware of us. He knows what is about to happen. He sees the mourning, the yearning for answers, and He hears the questioning *why.* Surely He weeps with us, just as He did with Martha and Mary. We must remember that ours is a God of miracles, and in His own time He will heal us. Most often that healing, that deliverance, will come in unexpected ways—that is the way of the Lord. Always, He is the means of bringing hope. The account of Lazarus reminds us of the truth that hope can come forth unexpectedly out of dark places.

In our time it is the same. Every spring the Lord sends us His visual reminder, "If you believed . . . you would see." Holy Week begins with this coming forth. From very dark places white blossoms burst forth out of their winter cocoons, yellow daffodils and pink tulips break through the dark soil, and the earth becomes new again. The blooms are a reminder of life after death, of hope after despair, of grace bursting forth from the darkness. Spring comes again, and in the midst of darkness, hope returns.

Take a minute to reflect on your own life. What binds you and confines you to the darkness? Whether it be sorrow or sin, fear or frustration, depression or despair, we must remember that Calvary's cross has the power to overcome every darkness.

Oh, may our eyes be open to believe, to see the unexpected, to recognize the hope that is before us! For there will be dark days—moments when we are lonely or forgotten, days when we carry a burden so heavy we wonder if the weight of it will ever ease. Out of these dark places, hope will come forth. It always does. It always will.

I want my family to understand this truth, and often the most visual reminders are the greatest catalyst for learning to take place. So our first tradition of Easter begins with the darkest soil I can find and a handful of seeds. To begin this tradition, we talk about hope and the power it has to come forth out of the darkest of situations. Then we fill pots with soil almost to the brim. After we have spread the soil evenly, we cover the top with a full layer of wheat berries. Last, we place a thin layer of dark soil on top of the seeds. Then we begin to water. For the first three days we water the seeds every morning and every night. It isn't long before the green shoots begin to come forth from the black soil. Within a week the grass is long enough to tie a ribbon around and trim the top. My children watch the process daily. Every year we are surprised at how fast the grass grows—how quickly and unexpectedly the green breaks through the darkness. So it is with hope.

## THE TRADITION

# Recognize Unexpected Hope

**An Easter Hymn**

Be Still, My Soul

**A Story to Tell . . . A Lesson to Share**

Read John 11:1–46

What can you learn from the story of Lazarus? What does this story teach us about the hope the Savior can bring in the darkest moments of our lives?

**The Moment of Celebration**

In representation of the hope that springs forth out of dark places, spend an evening planting wheat baskets. You will need to purchase wheat berries from the bulk section in a health food store and a bag of planting soil. Next, find a pot that drains well. Put the dirt into the pot and pack it down. Carefully place the wheat berries on top of the dirt, completely covering the dirt with an entire layer of wheat berries. Place a tiny bit of dirt over the seeds to keep them moist when you water. Water the wheat morning and night for the first several days to make sure it stays moist. The wheat will begin to sprout from the dark soil in about three days. After a week or so you can clip it so that it remains shorter, or let it grow longer and tie a ribbon around the middle of the grass to give it strength. At that point the plant will require water about every three days. When the grass has grown and you have trimmed it up, you might consider dropping the pot off secretly on somebody's porch with a message of hope.

*Lazarus reminds us of*
*the unexpected hope that will spring forth*
*from the darkest moments of our lives.*

*He hath sent me to bind up the brokenhearted . . .*

Isaiah 61:1, KJV

TWO

# SIMON

The night that began with the mockery of a kiss had been filled with pain. Excruciating pain. The weight of it settled right into His heart. Darkness fell, bringing with it first betrayal and then torture. He was surrounded by those who mocked and questioned Him. Their intent was to destroy Him, whatever the cost. After spending all night with the enemy, Jesus must have sorrowed over the knowledge that there was no one on His side.

Morning came with the possibility of reprieve. "I . . . have found no fault in this man . . . nothing worthy of death is done unto him. . . . Pilate therefore, willing to release Jesus, spake again to them. But they cried, saying, Crucify him, crucify him. And he said . . . , Why, what evil hath he done?" (Luke 23:14–15, 20–22, KJV).

*What evil had He done?* Feeding the multitudes? Raising the dead? Healing the blind, the lepers, and the lame? Did those things mean nothing to them—the loving kindness, the miracles, the blessings? When they looked back at the whole of His life, what He gave and taught and testified of, was it worthy of the cross? Luke writes that they were insistent with loud shouts, demanding that He be crucified (see Luke 23:23).

They wove a crown of thorns and placed it upon His head, and as they mocked Him, they spat on Him and smote Him. Then, finally, after a night with no sleep and a day filled with torture, He was led away to be crucified. Bruised and bleeding, He began to walk. "And as they led him away, they laid hold upon one Simon, a Cyrenian, coming out of the country, and on him they laid the cross, that he might bear it after Jesus" (Luke 23:26, KJV).

When I think of Simon the Cyrenian, who came out of the country, I picture a man of very humble means. A passerby. Simon may not have had much to offer to the world, and yet his name is recorded in a scriptural account that will stand as a witness of his actions forever. Throughout time he will be remembered as a man who was willing to offer an act of goodness in a moment of great need, to take a compassionate detour. Simon couldn't take away the pain that lay ahead. But for a small moment he could help bear the burden, even shoulder it, and for that moment the Savior did not suffer alone.

In the midst of greatest pain, sometimes comfort comes from simply knowing that we don't walk the road alone. A favorite quote of mine speaks of this sentiment: "I'm glad to think I've helped you a little when you came to a hard place, for the most any one of us may do for another is to smooth the road" (Myrtle Reed, *Old Rose and Silver*, 314). There are people all around us who shoulder heavy burdens. Many nights find them lying awake, the weight of their burdens settling right into their hearts. Perhaps they feel as if the trials will destroy them.

Sadly, we can't take the pain away. But could we help shoulder the burden? What might we learn from Simon's example? Are we willing to give comfort to someone whose burden is heavy? Are we willing to help another person bear the load?

Sometimes I wonder why Mark made mention of this humble man's two sons, Alexander and Rufus, in his account. Their part in the story intrigues me. I wonder how old they were. I wonder if they watched their father bear the burden of heavy wood upon his shoulder. I wonder if in later years they asked their father to tell the story again about that day, the day he took upon him the cross of Jesus. I can't help but be reminded of the words in Matthew, "If anyone would come after me, he must deny himself and take up his cross and follow me" (Matthew 16:24, NIV).

The story of Simon speaks to my mother heart. At its very roots, it is the story of a father who humbly taught a powerful lesson by example to his two sons. It is a lesson that teaches of sacrifice, compassion, and love. I wanted to find a tradition that would remind my children of

Simon's story, a tradition that would help us all to become more aware of those around us who are shouldering heavy burdens and to find a way to help them bear their trials. Since Simon was from the country, I decided to look for something that would represent humble circumstances and the service that comes from personal sacrifice. After many days I settled on a spool of jute—the thin, inexpensive rope that can be found at any hardware store. We tied the jute around our wrists with a simple knot in the middle. We called it a "forget knot," and it became a reminder that we needed to look outside of ourselves to find those who might be struggling and then to act. To take a compassionate detour. To *forget not*.

Perhaps you could remember that in the midst of greatest pain, sometimes comfort comes from simply knowing that you don't walk the road alone, that someone is there beside you to help shoulder the load.

To bear you up.

## THE TRADITION

**An Easter Hymn**

Nearer, My God, to Thee

**A Story to Tell . . . A Lesson to Share**

Read the story of Simon of Cyrene in Matthew 27:32, Mark 15: 21, and Luke 23:26

What can you learn from the story of Simon? What does this story teach us about the importance of bearing the burdens of another?

**The Moment of Celebration**

When I remember Simon of Cyrene I try to remember that what he had to offer in a moment of great need was his service—his ability to shoulder a burden. His service did not come at great cost, but rather great sacrifice. Could you find a compassionate detour sometime this week? Could you offer service that does not come at great cost, but might require sacrifice on your part? Remember that Simon of Cyrene was possibly a man of humble means. To remind yourself of his act of service, perhaps you could purchase a simple strand of inexpensive string and tie it around your wrist. Maybe you will tie a simple "forget knot" right in the center. Let it remind you to watch for people who are bearing a heavy burden—to forget them not. Then find a way to help them shoulder their load.

~

*Simon exemplifies what it is to bear another's*
*burden so that it might be light.*
*He reminds us that although we can't*
*take away what lies ahead,*
*we can help shoulder the burden*
*for a while along the way.*

*To proclaim liberty to the captives,*
*and the opening of the prison*
*to them that are bound.*

ISAIAH 61:1, KJV

# THREE

# JOSEPH AND NICODEMUS

There is a phrase that has intrigued me since I began studying the story of Joseph of Arimathea and Nicodemus. It is a phrase with two different meanings depending on the situation you are in. I wonder which of the two meanings you would think of first. The phrase is *giving up*. What is the first thought that comes to your mind?

Is *giving up* what you feel like doing after a really bad day? Does it define a moment when you want to quit, surrender, yield, submit, or back down? Or did something entirely different come to mind?

Is *giving up* what you do when you offer something that is precious? Could to *give up* mean to sacrifice, devote, or dedicate? If that is true, then perhaps to *give up* means to *offer heavenward*.

Joseph of Arimathea was a member of the Jewish Sanhedrin, the high court in Israel. He was a rich man and a secret disciple of Jesus. Nicodemus was a Pharisee and leader who came to visit Jesus late one night. He was also a member of the Sanhedrin, which was a group that hated Jesus. But Joseph and Nicodemus had each experienced a change of heart, and it was this change of heart that gave them an understanding of what it truly meant to *give up*. Their personal experience with the Savior is a witness of this understanding.

It was after the death of Christ that Joseph of Arimathea, "being a disciple of Jesus, *but secretly for fear of the Jews*, besought Pilate that he might take away the body of Jesus: and Pilate gave him leave. He came therefore, and took the body of Jesus. And there came also

Nicodemus, *which at the first came to Jesus by night,* and brought a mixture of myrrh and aloes, about an hundred pound weight. Then took they the body of Jesus, and wound it in linen clothes with the spices, as the manner of the Jews is to bury. Now in the place where he was crucified there was a garden; and in the garden *a new sepulchre,* wherein was never man yet laid" (John 19:38–41, KJV).

It is the giving up that captures my heart in this account. Giving up of the secrecy to care for the body. Giving up of the myrrh and aloes—which must have come at great cost. Giving up of their time. Giving up of the tomb. In my mind's eye I see two men, turned disciples, who risked mockery and ridicule as they gently cared for the body of their Lord. These men knew what it was to give up. To offer heavenward.

In the first place, they gave up their pride. When they came together after the crucifixion, their belief in Jesus, which had been kept secret and hidden, had to be made manifest in the open. Together these two men took the body of Jesus and laid it in a tomb, at great risk to their safety and reputation. These men chose Christ, even though it might have meant losing all that they had attained in the world. This giving up came as a result of dedication.

Second, they gave up their possessions—new linen, myrrh, aloes, and an unused tomb. This giving up came as a result of their devotion. It was a giving up that spoke of sacrifice.

I think of those few hours before the Sabbath began and I can't help but imagine the tenderness with which they carefully prepared the body with the linen and incense before placing it into the new sepulcher. I wonder if they walked home with empty hands and aching hearts once their work was finished. In their giving up they had given all they had to offer. It was a gift born of sacrifice, which is the greatest gift that can be given.

Amidst their careful preparations, was there any idea of what would take place at that garden spot in three days' time? After their offering heavenward, after the giving up, after the stone had been rolled into place, did they question if the emptiness in their hearts would ever become full again? They couldn't possibly have foreseen the joy that would soon fill the empty space that had been carved out in preparation by their grief. Did they have any inkling that after the giving up and after the grieving they would experience firsthand the gift that would console every grief?

We don't know.

But we do know this: there was One who surely watched that moment of tender devotion and dedication. One who had been willing to give up everything in their behalf, *and in ours*. One who performed the ultimate gift born of sacrifice, which is the greatest gift ever given.

In three days' time the linens that had been given up would be left folded and no longer used. The sweet scent of incense that had been given up would linger no more. And the emptiness of the tomb would become a testament of what *Jesus* had given up. Offered heavenward. Sacrificed. The empty tomb would become a witness of His gift.

Do you know what it is to feel empty? Have the circumstances of life ever taken so much from you that it feels as if your whole soul has been carved out? There is One who can fill the empty places—Jesus Christ, the Holy One of Israel, the Messiah, the Son of God. He is the Anointed One—He who came to preach good tidings and to bind up the brokenhearted. The One who proclaims liberty to the captives and opens the prisons of those who are bound. He who offers comfort to those that mourn, who gives unto them beauty for ashes, and the oil of joy for mourning. He is the Savior who brings the garment of praise for the spirit of heaviness (see Isaiah 61:1–3).

He fills the empty places until they are full.

Jesus Christ gave up His life for us. Are we willing to follow His example? Could we choose daily to *give up* our lives for Jesus? Could our hearts become more devoted? Could our lives become more dedicated?

When we think of the story of Joseph and Nicodemus, we must remember that their sacrifice, their giving up, came as a result of their dedication and their devotion to what they believed. Some of the sweetest moments of giving up come from our willingness to share our deepest beliefs.

I will never forget one early spring evening. It had been a hard day. A friend in my neighborhood had been struggling. I was in charge of planning a youth group activity that evening, but I couldn't get my struggling friend out of my thoughts. As we gathered together, I shared the story of my friend with the girls I was with. I asked if they had any idea how we might lift her spirits. After brainstorming for a while, the girls came up with some ideas: *We could share with her what we believe about Jesus Christ to strengthen her. We could write down scriptures and quotes about Him. We could roll up those papers individually and place them in plastic Easter eggs and hang them secretly from that big tree in her front yard. We could help her remember to believe.*

So we did. We found quotes and scriptures and words that would help this friend, during a difficult time in her life, to believe in the healing Jesus Christ offers. We wrote them down and then rolled them up and placed them carefully in lots and lots of plastic Easter eggs. Then we drove over to her house. As quietly and secretly as we could, we tied those eggs filled with belief all over the tree in her front yard . . . from the very top branches to the very bottom. On that evening I watched those girls walk home with empty hands and full hearts. Together they had given my friend everything they had to offer—a witness of their belief in Jesus Christ. It was a gift that testified of His sacrifice, the greatest gift ever given. I knew that their giving up would allow my friend to experience the gift that could console her grief.

I drove past her house the next morning, and my heart filled with hope. The tree that had not yet started blooming was bursting with color—eggs of all different shades of spring hung from the branches. It was a testimony tree. A tree filled with the belief of a handful of disciples who were devoted to the Lord.

## THE TRADITION

### *Give Up*

**An Easter Hymn**

How Great Thou Art

**A Story to Tell . . . A Lesson to Share**

Read Mark 14:1–9 and John 19:38–41

What can you learn from the story of Joseph of Arimathea and Nicodemus? What do their stories teach us about giving up, or offering heavenward? Why might giving come as a result of your devotion to your belief in Christ?

**The Moment of Celebration**

Consider creating a testimony tree for someone you know who is struggling. There are a couple of ways you could do this. Perhaps you could carefully poke a hole with a needle at the top and bottom of a fresh egg.

Carefully blow out the yolk and the white of the egg into your sink. Then gently write one word that reminds you of Jesus Christ with white crayon on the egg before you dip it into dye. Once you pull it from the dye, the egg should be completely colored except for the letters of the word. When all your eggs are dry, carefully hang them with twine from tree branches. Another idea is to take a few minutes to have each member of your family write down his or her testimony of Jesus Christ. Take time to find quotes or scriptures that testify of Christ. Fold up the pieces of paper and place them into several plastic Easter eggs. Then hang the eggs with fishing line from a tree in your own yard or in the yard of someone in need.

*Joseph of Arimathea and Nicodemus*
*remind us that devotion, dedication, and sacrifice*
*will sometimes require giving up*
*in an effort to offer heavenward.*

*To comfort all that mourn;*
*to appoint unto them that mourn in Zion,*
*to give unto them beauty for ashes,*
*the oil of joy for mourning.*

Isaiah 61:2–3, KJV

FOUR

# THE WOMEN

When my son returned home after living in Serbia for several months, he told me about an Easter tradition he had experienced there. It is a tradition that celebrates the witness of women, and that is why it left such an impression on my heart.

After World War II came to an end, many people in Eastern European countries were not allowed to attend church services. The Communist Party taught the children that there was not a God. However, not wanting their grandchildren to grow up without a knowledge of

41

the Savior, the grandmothers would teach the children about Jesus within the walls of their own homes. Then, every year at Easter, the families would attend a midnight service. When they returned home, they would stay up all night long talking about Jesus and decorating red Easter eggs. For the people in Serbia, eggs symbolized the eternal life of Jesus. According to some legends, the white eggs Mary left at her son's tomb as a sacrifice turned red after His resurrection. These red eggs hold deep meaning for the people of Serbia.

My son explained that the morning after the midnight service, as soon as the sun had risen, the people would have a huge breakfast. Then they would go from door to door and visit each of their neighbors. As each door was opened, they would say, "Christ has risen," and the person at the door would answer, "Indeed He has risen." Then the person would give the guests at the door a red egg. The red egg meant good luck. It was common for a family to choose one red egg and display it until Easter came again the next year.

Although Christians in Serbia are now allowed to

worship publicly, much of this tradition still stands. It is not uncommon to see a red egg displayed prominently in a Serbian house long after Easter has passed. This egg is often called "the housekeeper," and it is supposed to guard the house until the next Easter. I love the imagery in this tradition—the grandmothers teaching, the white eggs that turned to red in memory of the sacrifice, the decorating of eggs every single year as a reminder.

The Easter story is filled with the witnesses of women. Several of their stories are mentioned within the days that surround the crucifixion of Jesus Christ. One of these stories is a scene that took place on Calvary's hill. We can't picture the scene on Calvary without considering the women who were there. "Near the cross of Jesus stood his mother, his mother's sister, Mary the wife of Clopas, and Mary Magdalene" (John 19:25, NIV).

*Near the cross of Jesus stood His mother.* Have you ever wondered what emotions filled Mary's heart that day? Surely she focused on the past memories she had of watching her son, the master teacher, as He taught multitudes of people. She must have pondered on the

43

miracles—His hands had been the means of healing the sick, raising the dead, calming the sea. Did she weep over the fact that one of His closest friends had chosen to betray Him; that those who had once honored Him had decided to crucify Him; that above all else He had chosen to follow His Father's will? In that moment of sorrow and anguish, as she saw the crown of thorns on His head, the nails in His hands, and her son there on the cross, did she weep? She could not possibly have foreseen the feelings that would enter her heart in the moment when the tomb would be found empty or when the disciples she revered would testify boldly, "He lives." I can't help but wonder, in the agony of that afternoon, if she remembered that sacred and still night in Bethlehem when she watched over her sleeping, swaddled son. Mary, who had been there at the beginning, stood by Him at the end. John tells us that one of the Lord's last thoughts was for His mother. To me, this poignant image is a testament of the power of a mother's love.

Those final moments were too much for a mother's heart to bear alone . . . they must have been. How grateful she must have been for a sweet sister, Mary the wife of Clopas, who came to support her—to carry her through. I picture her there, Mary's sister, with her quiet strength, her unyielding support, her devotion. May we remember the silent lesson she taught—in moments of greatest agony a sister can provide enabling strength.

And then there was Mary Magdalene. She had had the privilege of coming to know and love the Savior. Perhaps she was a dear friend, even a close confidante. We do not know much about this Mary, but we do know that she was the first person to see the risen Lord. I have often wondered why. Was her faith the most sufficient? Was she the most prepared to receive the Savior? Did Christ know she would recognize Him when He called her name because she had before? We do not know, but we do know this—she went to the tomb early one morning after Christ had died, and here an important lesson was learned.

She went seeking the Savior. In her hour of greatest need, in deep despair and longing for answers, she did what she had been taught to do—she turned to Christ.

Weeping, she sat outside the tomb. A man approached her and asked, "Woman, why weepest thou? whom seekest thou?" (John 20:15, KJV). And Mary, thinking he was the gardener, asked if he had taken Jesus's body.

Mary was a woman who had a great level of knowledge pertaining to the teachings of Christ. She had come to know the Savior during His ministry on the earth. So we might wonder why she did not at first recognize this man as Jesus Christ.

Perhaps it was because on that Easter morning Mary's level of understanding was that Christ was dead. Weeping in frustration and sorrow, she sought to find Him. She did not recognize His voice at first because in her mind it was not possible. But then—it was! In that moment, Mary's testimony of Christ increased. She had reached a new level of understanding.

How often do we come to a point in our lives when we are comfortable and confident in our relationship with Christ? We may go forward for a time serving and learning. Then, inevitably, a trial will come that will test our knowledge. It may even cause us to question what we believe and know of the Lord. At these times we realize that our testimony is never stagnant. Trials provide an opportunity for us to seek the Savior. As we prove Him, we gain more understanding and knowledge. We come to know Him in a way we might not have before.

Mary did not recognize the Savior until He called her name. "A moment's pause, and He spake her name in those well-remembered accents. . . . She could not mistake the Voice" (Edersheim, *Life and Times*, 2:635). Then, all of a sudden, light and understanding came. She had reached a new level of knowledge: Christ is risen; He lives; there is life after death. He had conquered the grave and was victorious. The Savior stood by her in her moment of learning. He waited patiently until she was ready, and then He taught.

Just like the experience Mary Magdalene had at the tomb that Easter morning, we each can have personal experiences with the Lord. He will stand by us, and He will call us by name. In those moments, just like Mary, our knowledge of Him will increase . . . our testimony of Him will grow . . . and because of Him our lives will never be the same.

These three experiences remind us how personal and how meaningful a relationship with Jesus Christ can be. Mary His mother stood by Him, while her sister, Mary the wife of Clopas, stood by her. Mary Magdalene sought the Savior in her time of need. Their stories remind us that we too can have those tender, one-on-one experiences with the Savior. Perhaps we could share our witness of these experiences with our own children and grandchildren.

One Easter my husband and I invited our children's grandmother to dinner. Before we sat down to eat, we talked about the story of the grandmothers in Serbia who taught their grandchildren about Jesus Christ. I placed one red egg in the middle of the table. Then we asked our grandmother to share her feelings about Jesus Christ. My children sat transfixed. A beautiful spirit filled the room. It was an evening I will always remember.

## The Tradition
# *Bear Witness*

**An Easter Hymn**

I Know That My Redeemer Lives

**A Story to Tell . . . A Lesson to Share**

Read the account of the three women at the cross in John 19:25–27, and the story of Mary Magdalene in John 20:11–18

Think about these three women: One bore witness with her presence, one bore witness with her support, and one bore witness with her testimony of the risen Lord. What do you learn from these three stories?

**The Moment of Celebration**

Spend an evening dying Easter eggs and talking about what it means to stand as a witness for Jesus Christ. Focus on how every testimony is unique, fragile, and worth taking care of. Discuss why the egg represents the eternal life of Jesus. You might consider dying several eggs red. Perhaps you will display one of those eggs prominently in your home as a reminder that Christ has risen.

To make a beautiful red dye, use the skins of fifteen yellow onions. (Yes, yellow!) Place the onion skins in a saucepan with 3 to 4 cups of water and 2 tablespoons of vinegar. Bring to a boil; boil gently for 30 minutes. Let cool to room temperature. Wash 6 uncooked eggs; place in onion water. Return pan to heat and simmer about 15 minutes. Remove from heat, leaving eggs in the water. Let sit for 20 minutes, then place pan with eggs and dye in the refrigerator overnight to achieve a deep red. Remove eggs from dye, let them dry completely, then polish with olive oil.

∽

*Mary Magdalene, Mary the Mother of Jesus,*
*and Mary the Wife of Clopas*
*remind us that our personal experiences with the Lord*
*will create testimonies that are unique, fragile,*
*and worth sharing with those we love.*

*. . . the garment of praise for the spirit of heaviness.*

ISAIAH 61:3, KJV

# FIVE

# THOMAS

Every time the snow fell, we pulled out the old blue shovel and piled it all up in the front garden next to the sidewalk. One year, the pile grew higher and higher as winter stretched on. It was the highest pile of snow that our little flower garden had ever borne. The weight of it was thick and heavy. I began to wonder if it would ever melt. I knew that there were lily bulbs waiting to bloom under that heavy burden. As the winter stretched on, I began to worry that those lilies wouldn't ever grow. *Could anything flourish under that thick blanket of cold?*

But way down deep in the bottom of my heart I believed that they would. They always had before. Every spring the sun comes out, bringing with it warmth to overcome the coldness, and the lilies come forth in all their glory.

For me, lilies symbolize belief. They are like a promise of the beauty that springs forth when the sun comes out again.

Lilies remind me of the story of Thomas. This story is a part of Easter that I don't ever forget. The Lord had come to visit the apostles after His death, but for some reason Thomas wasn't there. The others, after seeing Him, bore testimony to Thomas, "We have seen the Lord" (John 20:25, KJV).

For eight days Thomas waited. I wonder if the anxiousness in his heart grew higher and higher as the days stretched on. Would the Lord remember Thomas? Would He come back to visit him? The weight of that thought must have been thick and heavy. Perhaps he was fearful that the Lord wouldn't come again; maybe he thought he had missed his chance to see the Lord after His death. It is hard for belief to thrive under that heavy burden. We don't know the circumstances of the questioning, but we do know that Thomas's heart filled with doubt, "Except I shall see in his hands the print of the nails, and put my finger into the print of the nails, and thrust my hand into his side, *I will not believe*" (John 20:25, KJV).

Then came Jesus.

And He said to Thomas, "Reach hither thy finger, and behold my hands; and reach hither thy hand, and thrust it into my side: and be not faithless, *but believing*" (John 20:27, KJV).

Oh, how I love that moment. The Savior knew the fears and the deepest longings of Thomas's heart—to see, to feel, to believe. Jesus didn't ignore Thomas's doubt or his questioning. He invited Thomas to reach, to have a personal experience, so that he could discover the answer himself. He knew that experience would allow Thomas to believe.

The Son had come again.

"Then Jesus told him, Because you have seen me, you have believed; blessed are those who have not seen and yet have believed" (John 20:29, NIV).

The story of Thomas reminds us of the importance of believing. We live in troubled times. Sometimes the weight of our circumstance is thick and heavy. It is hard for belief to thrive under that heavy burden. Like Thomas, we may wonder if it is worth allowing a belief in the Lord to grow. On those days perhaps we could remember the lesson taught by the Lord during the Sermon on the Mount, "Consider the lilies of the field, how they grow" (Matthew 6:28, KJV). There is an important reminder here: lilies grow. Every spring it is the same. No matter the circumstance, even with all the coldness and uncertainty in the world around them, they grow. They come up. They bloom again. It is a belief that we can hold on to.

Lilies represent the spiritual meaning of Easter and are sometimes called the "white-robed apostles of hope." They symbolize life, purity, hope, faith, renewal, promise, and remembrance. Lilies testify of the resurrection of Jesus

Christ and the hope of life everlasting. They symbolize a deep and abiding belief in the resurrection of the Lord.

The lily is a beautiful reminder that we must continue to believe even in a world that is uncertain. There will be moments of waiting. In those moments we may question everything we have built our trust on; perhaps we will even experience doubt. There will be times when all that we hope for seems bound by unyielding constraints. If we are not careful, we can doubt ourselves into a place that is cold, lonely, and full of heartache. Sometimes wavering thoughts turn bitter, hearts grow cold, and the seed of faith lies dormant. In such times, we must cling to our belief in Jesus Christ. In our moments of doubt, He stands waiting with open arms. If we open our hearts, the Son will come and bring with Him the peace that will lead to a deep and abiding belief. When we are in need of a reminder of this truth, we just need to consider the lilies. With springtime comes the promise that the lilies will bloom again. They always have—they always will.

## THE TRADITION
*Believe*

**An Easter Hymn**

How Deep the Father's Love for Us

**A Story to Tell . . . A Lesson to Share**

Read John 20:25–29

What can you learn from the story of Thomas? How can that knowledge help you hold onto belief through times of doubt or discouragement? How might it help you to strengthen the belief of someone you know who is struggling?

**The Moment of Celebration**

Stop by a floral shop and purchase a bouquet of lilies to display in your home throughout this season as a reminder that a deep and abiding belief in Jesus Christ can bring peace and sustain us through every moment of doubt. Do you know someone who could use a reminder of that truth? Perhaps you could drop off a bouquet of these "white-robed apostles of hope" with a testimony of your belief in Jesus Christ.

∽

*Thomas reminds us*
*that clinging to our belief in the Lord*
*will sustain us in moments of doubt*
*and bring peace in a world of uncertainty.*

*I will direct their work in truth . . .*

Isaiah 61:8, KJV

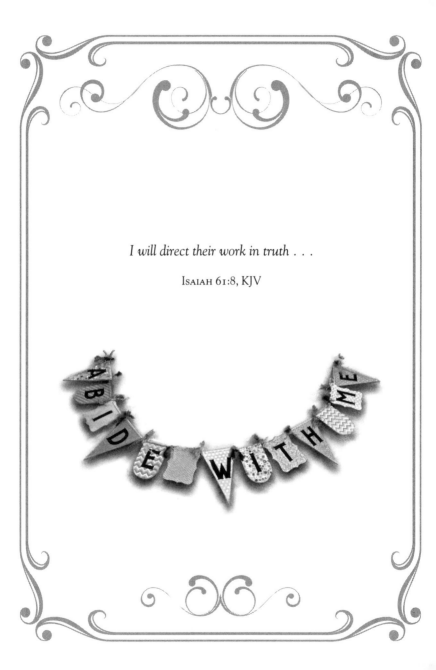

# SIX

# TWO DISCIPLES ON THE ROAD TO EMMAUS

They left the city in the early afternoon of a spring day just after the crucifixion—two disciples traveling to Emmaus, talking of all that had happened as they walked. For almost two hours they traveled, passing country houses along the way. Just beyond a dreary, rocky region, they climbed a path with a stream running alongside, passing through orchards of orange and lemon trees, olive groves, and shady nooks. In all, their walk probably encompassed six or seven miles, and surely every mile was filled with conversation about Jesus Christ—the memories, the miracles, and the mystery of the empty tomb (see Edersheim, *Life and Times*, 2:639).

Somewhere along the way, a stranger joined them on the road. The men were so caught up in conversation they did not at first acknowledge Him. The stranger asked why they were so sad. Cleopas answered by asking if the man was a stranger and wondering how it was that he did not know of the things that had happened in Jerusalem. "What things?" the stranger asked. So they began to tell the story, laying out the details and pouring out their hearts. They told of how Jesus of Nazareth had come, who was mighty in deed and in word, how the chief priests and rulers had delivered Him to be crucified, and how they had trusted that it had been He who would redeem Israel. It was in this moment that their pouring out turned to testimony, "And what is more, it is the third day since this took place" (Luke 24:19, 21, NIV). They spoke of certain women who had been to the sepulcher and returned astonished, and women who had seen angels who testified that Jesus was alive. Then they talked of two men who ran to the sepulcher and saw that it was empty, "but him they saw not" (Luke 24:24, KJV).

There must have been a silence hanging in the air in the pause that followed. The astonishment, the desperate hope, the wonder—all of it too great to put into words. It was in that moment that the stranger began to speak. His words were filled with scriptural verses that defined the mission of Jesus Christ. By now it was almost evening. Having reached a fork in the road that signified they had arrived in the village that was their destination, the disciples asked the stranger to tarry with them. "Abide with us: for it is toward evening, and the day is far spent" (Luke 24:29, KJV).

So the stranger went with them to the home. It was as they partook of a simple meal that the eyes of their understanding were opened. They suddenly recognized the resurrected Lord, "and they knew him; and he vanished out of their sight" (Luke 24:31, KJV). Realization dawned in that instant: "Were not our hearts burning within us while he talked with us on the road and opened the Scriptures to us?" (Luke 24:32, NIV).

It was the next day, when they had returned to Jerusalem and all the disciples were together, that Jesus returned again. "Then opened he their understanding, that they might understand the scriptures" (Luke 24:45, KJV).

The lesson from the story of these two disciples is simple but profound—it is through the scriptures that a disciple comes to know and recognize the Lord. This lesson is just as true today as it was two thousand years ago. If you want to know Jesus Christ, you must turn to the scriptures.

There are so many ways to make the scriptures part of your Easter celebration. You might consider reading one chapter of John or another of the Gospels every day for a period leading up to Easter. You might make a Bible study of all the events that happened during the Holy Week leading up to the crucifixion and resurrection of Christ. One of my favorite personal traditions is to come up with a forty-day course of reading and study to be completed on Easter morning. I enjoy the forty days of spiritual preparation as I study verses that testify of the life and teachings of Jesus Christ.

In our family we have a favorite tradition that reminds us of the importance of the scriptures during the Easter season. Every year we hang a scripture banner. The banner is simple; it is made of triangles cut out of brightly colored paper. Each of the triangles has one black letter pasted in the middle. The banner reads, "Abide with Me." It is a visual reminder of the personal experience that took place between the Savior and the two disciples on the road to Emmaus. During the week we celebrate this tradition, we each ponder our favorite scriptures about the Savior. As we remember them, we write them down on small pieces of paper and hang them from the banner in between the triangles. By the end of the week our "Abide with Me" banner has become a gathering place for our favorite scriptures about Jesus Christ.

Every follower of Christ will ultimately travel his or her own road to Emmaus. There will be days of sorrow and times of sadness. Hopefully, along that road we will turn to the scriptures and experience those moments when our hearts burn within us as we read. There will be verses that stand out to us, and we will be reminded that we are not forgotten of the Lord. The messages contained on those holy pages will leave an impression on our hearts, and as they settle there, perhaps we will echo the words of a favorite hymn:

> *Abide with me! fast falls the eventide;*
> *The darkness deepens. Lord, with me abide!*
> *When other helpers fail and comforts flee,*
> *Help of the helpless, oh, abide with me!*
> (Henry F. Lyte, 1847)

## THE TRADITION
# *Draw Near*

**An Easter Hymn**

Come, Thou Fount of Every Blessing

**A Story to Tell . . . A Lesson to Share**

Read the account of the two disciples walking on the road to Emmaus, found in Luke 24:13–32

Why do you think the two men recognized the Savior when He opened the scriptures to them along the way? Is the same true for us today?

**The Moment of Celebration**

Create your own scripture banner. Use the phrase "Abide with Me," or think of another short scripture phrase that testifies of Jesus Christ. Hang it somewhere in your home where people will pass by it frequently. Cut out small strips of scrapbook paper and place them in a basket near your banner. As the days go by, encourage those who pass by the banner to add their favorite scripture about Jesus Christ there.

~⊃

*The Disciples on the Road to Emmaus*
*remind us that as we turn to the scriptures*
*our hearts will burn within,*
*we will be led to recognize the Lord,*
*and His Spirit will abide with us.*

*I will greatly rejoice in the Lord,*
*my soul shall be joyful in my God;*
*for he hath clothed me with the garments of salvation,*
*he hath covered me with the robe of righteousness.*

<small>ISAIAH 61:10, KJV</small>

# SEVEN

# JESUS CHRIST

I am a collector of old religious books. I love the language, the worn pages, and the cracked bindings. Most of these antique books come with handwritten inscriptions on the inside of the front cover identifying the owner and the date the book was purchased. One of my favorite volumes was owned by Reverend Wilmond A. Warner of Barton, Vermont. The book is entitled *The Life and Times of Jesus the Messiah,* by Alfred Edersheim. The wonderful thing about having a book once owned by a Reverend is that you get to read the markings and notes he left behind on the pages.

The book shares the events of Christ's royal entry into Jerusalem: "Everywhere the tramp of their feet, and the shout of their acclamations brought men, women, and children into the streets and on the housetops. The City was moved, and from mouth to mouth the question passed among the eager crowed of curious onlookers: 'Who is He?' And the multitude answered—not, this is Israel's Messiah-King, but: 'This is Jesus the Prophet of Nazareth of Galilee.' And so up into the Temple! He alone was silent and sad among this excited multitude, the marks of the tears He had wept over Jerusalem still on His cheek. He spake not, but only looked round about upon all things, as if to view the field on which He was to suffer and die. And now the shadows of evening were creeping up; and, weary and sad, He once more returned with the twelve disciples to the shelter and rest of Bethany" (Edersheim, *Life and Times*, 2:373).

Underneath this passage appears a note, carefully

written in beautiful script, that I love: "Wilmond Warner—
Evening—March 31, 1928—Tomorrow is Palm Sunday."

When I read that quote and then the inscription underneath, I know something about Reverend Wilmond A. Warner of Barton, Vermont: He was a man who knew what it meant to prepare his heart for the High Holiday of Easter.

This preparing is a common theme of Easter. Luke writes, "And he sent Peter and John, saying, Go and *prepare* us the passover, that we may eat" (Luke 22:8, KJV; emphasis added). The preparation was a process. It would require finding a man bearing a pitcher of water, following him to his home, and asking if he would provide a guestchamber. Then Jesus says, "And he shall shew you a large upper room furnished: *there make ready*" (Luke 22:12, KJV; emphasis added). It was in that room that He would give them a cup and broken bread, saying, "This do in *remembrance* of me" (Luke 22:19; emphasis added).

First, make ready, and then, remember. As Easter approaches, we too must prepare. Make ready your heart.

Make ready your home. Make ready your celebration. And then . . . remember.

In our family we celebrate Easter Sunday by gathering together for dinner. It is a meal in which we lay out our finest for the Lord—goblets, china plates, and linen napkins. In the center of the table there is a simple wrought-iron stand. Eight scrolls hang from the stand, rolled up and tied with beautiful white ribbons. Each scroll contains a segment of the Easter Sermon of St. John Chrysostom.

Before the dinner begins, we each take one of the scrolls, and then we take turns reading. I love this sermon. I was introduced to it by a dear friend. It is a reminder for me of the parable of the laborers in the vineyard in Matthew 20:1–16, the parable of the prodigal son in Luke 15:11–32, and the words of Isaiah in chapter 14 of his writings. The sermon helps us to remember.

## THE EASTER SERMON

If anyone is devout and a lover of God,
let them enjoy this beautiful and radiant festival.
If anyone is a grateful servant,
let them, rejoicing, enter into the joy of his Lord.

If anyone has wearied themselves in fasting,
let them now receive recompense.
If anyone has labored from the first hour,
let them today receive the just reward.
If anyone has come at the third hour,
with thanksgiving let them feast.
If anyone has arrived at the sixth hour,
let them have no misgivings; for they shall suffer no
    loss.
If anyone has delayed until the ninth hour,
let them draw near without hesitation.
If anyone has arrived even at the eleventh hour,
let them not fear on account of tardiness.
For the Master is gracious and receives the last even
    as the first;
He gives rest to him that comes at the eleventh hour,
just as to him who has labored from the first.
He has mercy upon the last and cares for the first;
to the one He gives, and to the other He is gracious.
He both honors the work and praises the intention.
Enter all of you, therefore, into the joy of our Lord,
and, whether first or last, receive your reward.
O rich and poor, one with another, dance for joy!

O you ascetics and you negligent, celebrate the day!

You that have fasted and you that have disregarded
the fast, rejoice today!

The table is rich-laden: feast royally, all of you!

The calf is fatted: let no one go forth hungry!

Let all partake of the feast of faith. Let all receive the
riches of goodness.

Let no one lament their poverty, for the universal
kingdom has been revealed.

Let no one mourn their transgressions, for pardon has
dawned from the grave.

Let no one fear death, for the Saviour's death has set
us free.

He that was taken by death has annihilated it!

He descended into Hades and took Hades captive!

He embittered it when it tasted His flesh! And antici-
pating this, Isaiah exclaimed: "*Hades was embittered
when it encountered Thee in the lower regions.*"

It was embittered, for it was abolished!

It was embittered, for it was mocked!

It was embittered, for it was purged!

It was embittered, for it was despoiled!

It was embittered, for it was bound in chains!

It took a body and came upon God!

It took earth and encountered Heaven!

It took what it saw, but crumbled before what it had
not seen!

O death, where is thy sting?

O Hades, where is thy victory?

Christ is risen, and you are overthrown!

Christ is risen, and the demons are fallen!

Christ is risen, and the angels rejoice!

Christ is risen, and life reigns!

Christ is risen, and not one dead remains in a tomb!

For Christ, being raised from the dead,

has become the first-fruits of them that have slept.

To Him be glory and might unto the ages of ages.

Amen.

On this Easter day, it is my prayer that you will find a
way to offer up your finest to the Lord. Make ready your
heart. Remember.

Rejoice in Him.

## The Tradition

*Rejoice!*

**An Easter Hymn**

Christ the Lord Is Risen Today

**A Story to Tell . . . A Lesson to Share**

Read the parable of the laborers in the vineyard in Matthew 20:1–16, the parable of the prodigal son in Luke 15:11–32, and Isaiah 14

**The Moment of Celebration**

Find a way today to celebrate Jesus Christ. Perhaps you will prepare a beautiful Easter meal. Maybe you will wake up early and watch the sun rise. You might consider reading the Easter Sermon, or you might find a different passage of scripture or form of poetry that offers words to express your deepest gratitude for the Savior. Today, find a way to offer up your finest in celebration of the Lord.

~⌒~

*Jesus Christ through His sacrifice*
*became our Redeemer,*
*the Holy One of Israel, our Savior.*
*On this day, rejoice in Him.*

# CONCLUSION

Easter is a holiday that we mark on our calendars on one Sunday every year, but in reality it is a celebration that should take place every day of our lives. The sacrifice and resurrection of our Lord merit more than just one high holiday a year; His is a gift that must be rejoiced in continually. We must not take it for granted. We must let it fill our hearts with hope.

In order to remember this lesson, perhaps we could consider two separate experiences that weren't included within the stories and traditions of this book. One took place in the hours just before Christ died, and the other took place just after He had risen.

You can't think back on the last few days and hours of the Savior's life and not be reminded of Judas. As much as we want to forget that Christ was betrayed by one of His closest friends, we can't. It is part of the story, and it teaches a powerful lesson. Judas was a disciple of Jesus Christ. He had witnessed miracles, heard the voice of the Lord, and even experienced His touch. However, at a crucial moment Judas laid all of that aside for thirty pieces of silver (see Luke 22:3–6, 47–49). His story leads to a question we must all ask ourselves: *Do I take for granted my testimony of the Lord?*

I don't want to.

Instead, I want to focus my attention on a story that happened just after the Savior had risen. I want to be more like Peter and John, running to the tomb after Mary told them it was empty (see John 20:1–10). I love the image of that moment—two disciples running with an abundance of hope that filled their faces and every fiber of their being. When given an invitation to come closer to Christ, to know more of Him, to celebrate Him, I want to consider the condition of my heart. I don't want to take for granted my testimony of the Savior and His suffering, death, and resurrection.

Instead, I want to come running.

Not just on Easter.

I want to rejoice in Him every day.

# SEVEN EASTER TRADITIONS

## LAZARUS

*reminds us of the unexpected hope that will spring forth
from the darkest moments of our lives.*

## SIMON

*exemplifies what it is to bear another's
burden so that it might be light.
He reminds us that although we can't
take away what lies ahead,
we can help shoulder the burden
for a while along the way.*

## JOSEPH OF ARIMATHEA AND NICODEMUS

*remind us that devotion, dedication, and sacrifice
will sometimes require giving up
in an effort to offer heavenward.*

## MARY MAGDALENE, MARY THE MOTHER OF JESUS, AND MARY THE WIFE OF CLOPAS

*remind us that our personal experiences with the Lord*
*will create testimonies that are unique, fragile,*
*and worth sharing with those we love.*

## THOMAS

*reminds us that clinging to our belief in the Lord*
*will sustain us in moments of doubt*
*and bring peace in a world of uncertainty.*

## THE DISCIPLES ON THE ROAD TO EMMAUS

*remind us that as we turn to the scriptures*
*our hearts will burn within,*
*we will be led to recognize the Lord,*
*and His Spirit will abide with us.*

## JESUS CHRIST

*through His sacrifice*
*became our Redeemer,*
*the Holy One of Israel, our Savior.*
*On this day, rejoice in Him.*

# SOURCES

Edersheim, Alfred. *The Life and Times of Jesus the Messiah*, 2 vols. New York: Longmans, Green, and Co., 1899.

Reed, Myrtle. *Old Rose and Silver*. New York: Grosset & Dunlap, 1909.

# ABOUT THE AUTHOR

EMILY BELLE FREEMAN'S writing reflects a deep love of the scriptures and a strong desire to share their application in modern-day life. She is the author of many books, including, most recently, *The Peter Potential: Discover the Life You Were Meant to Live*. Emily and her husband, Greg, are the parents of four children and live in Lehi, Utah.

For more ideas, visit achristcenteredeaster.com

Follow Emily at:
    www.dailyclosertochrist.com
    www.multiplygoodness.com